Original title:
Whirlwind of Feelings

Copyright © 2024 Creative Arts Management OÜ
All rights reserved.

Author: Maxwell Donovan
ISBN HARDBACK: 978-9916-88-944-2
ISBN PAPERBACK: 978-9916-88-945-9

Breathless in the Chaos

In the heart of the storm, we stand still,
Lost in the whirlwind, against our will.
Voices around us, a frantic race,
Seeking solace in this crowded space.

Stars flicker dimly, caught in the night,
Dreams whisper softly, just out of sight.
Moments like echoes, fade into gray,
We chase the silence, but it slips away.

Hands stretch out, grasping for calm,
In this tempestuous world, we seek a balm.
Breathless we wander, through shadows and light,
Searching for refuge, in endless flight.

But in the chaos, a heartbeat rings true,
A bond unbroken, connecting me and you.
Together we rise, though the world may fall,
In breathless chaos, love conquers all.

Torn Apart by Moments

In fleeting time we feel the strain,
Memories linger, stitched with pain.
Echoes of laughter now bittersweet,
Love once whole, now incomplete.

In quiet corners, shadows dwell,
Once bright hues have lost their spell.
Fragments scattered, hearts laid bare,
Each second passing, unaware.

Yet in the chaos, sparks ignite,
A flicker shines through darkest night.
Resilience rises from the dust,
In every fracture, hope is a must.

So hold the moments, brief yet grand,
Transform the hurt with a gentle hand.
As time moves on, we find our way,
Together, whole, come what may.

Shadows of Untold Stories

In twilight's grasp, secrets unfold,
Whispers linger, dreams retold.
Each heart harbors a silent plea,
Mysteries born, yet never free.

With every shadow, a tale waits,
Paths untraveled, uncertain fates.
Voices echo where silence grew,
Unseen battles fought, unacknowledged too.

Underneath the moon's soft light,
Hidden truths dare step from night.
Stories woven with threads of grace,
In the shadows, we find our place.

So listen close to the quiet sigh,
For every story has wings to fly.
The untold waits for eyes to see,
In each shadow, a voice set free.

Reverberations of Euphoria

In joyous bursts, the heart takes flight,
Moments spark like stars at night.
Laughter dances on the breeze,
A melody that puts us at ease.

Each heartbeat echoes, pure delight,
In warm embraces, souls ignite.
Colors blend in vibrant sway,
With every breath, we seize the day.

Yet joy teaches us to feel,
In every rise, the pain is real.
Reverberations touch our core,
Lighting paths we've walked before.

So let's embrace this fleeting grace,
In euphoria, we find our place.
For in the waves of joy, we see,
The beauty of life's tapestry.

Whispering Winds of Change

The winds arise with tales to tell,
Of shifting sands where dreams may dwell.
Each breeze carries a gentle nudge,
A call for growth, a timeless judge.

Leaves may fall, yet roots run deep,
In silence, the earth begins to weep.
Change weaves through with tender hands,
Transforming fears to hopeful plans.

Underneath the stars' soft glow,
New directions begin to show.
With whispered winds, we take the leap,
Embracing all, through loss and keep.

So let the winds of change embrace,
Guide us gently to our place.
In every shift, a world anew,
Awakening the hearts that grew.

The Rise and Fall

In shadows deep, the whispers call,
The echoes of the rise and fall.
With every peak, a valley waits,
A dance of fate that shifts and quakes.

The crowns we wear, the thorns we bear,
In glory's light, all hearts laid bare.
Yet softly fades the brightest light,
As twilight stalks the fleeting night.

Tornadoes of Hope

From silent dreams, a tempest brews,
A whirlwind tight, with vibrant hues.
It twists and turns, it bends the trees,
Amidst the chaos, hearts find ease.

In nature's grasp, we find our way,
Through swirling winds of night and day.
Each gust a push, a drive to soar,
In tornadoes of hope, we dare to explore.

Flickers in the Storm

A tempest rages, dark and wild,
Yet in the chaos, hope is filed.
Through rain and wind, a light does gleam,
A flicker bright, a fragile dream.

In every clash, a spark ignites,
A warmth that glimmers, soft as lights.
It whispers truths we hold so dear,
That even storms can bring us cheer.

Melodies in the Chaos

Amidst the noise, a song is found,
In every clash, a soaring sound.
The symphony of life plays on,
As order weaves with chaos drawn.

In every break, a rhythm beats,
On stormy paths, adventure greets.
Through trials faced and battles fought,
Melodies in chaos, dearly sought.

Vortex of Dreams

In the stillness of the night,
Whispers twist and turn,
Floating thoughts take flight,
In the mind, they burn.

Colors dance in shadows deep,
Fleeting visions swirl,
Secrets that the dreamers keep,
Lost in a timeless whirl.

Echoes of a distant call,
Through the mist they roam,
Cascading like a waterfall,
Guiding hearts back home.

In this realm where wishes thrive,
Hope and faith collide,
In the vortex, we arrive,
On a wondrous ride.

Symphony of Turmoil

Chords of chaos fill the air,
Notes of joy and pain,
Life's wild dance, a vibrant flare,
In the storm, we gain.

Melodies of heartache play,
Striking deep within,
A rhythm leads us far away,
Where the shadows spin.

In the clash of sound and silence,
Harmonies break free,
Finding strength in defiance,
Screaming out to be.

We rise and fall, an endless tune,
In this concert grand,
Through the chaos, we commune,
In the symphony, we stand.

Bliss and Bitter Winds

Whispers soften in the breeze,
Sweetness lingers long,
Yet shadows haunt with silent pleas,
In the heart, a song.

Golden rays of sunlit glee,
Chase the dark away,
While the winds of fate decree,
Some dreams won't stay.

In the balance of the light,
Hope and sorrow blend,
On a journey through the night,
Torn between to mend.

Still we dance on fragile ground,
Embracing both the highs,
For in every note we've found,
Beauty in the lies.

Heart's Tornado

Spin my thoughts like leaves in air,
Whirling with no end,
A tempest born from love's wild dare,
Breaks with every bend.

Caught within this swirling fate,
Passion's fierce embrace,
As desire and fear collate,
Match in perfect trace.

In the eye, a moment's peace,
Before the storm regains,
Yet in chaos, we find release,
Through the heart's refrains.

Tornado pulls, we twist and turn,
Seeking solid ground,
In the whirlwind, hearts still yearn,
Where true love is found.

Constellations in the Chaos

Stars gleam in the night sky,
Guiding lost souls with their light.
Amidst the storms of life's fight,
A spark of hope, shining bright.

Galaxies swirl in endless dance,
Whispers of fate in every glance.
In the madness, we take a chance,
To find love in a fleeting trance.

The Frenzy of Heartstrings

Heartbeats echo through the night,
Strings pulled tight in love's delight.
Emotions clash, a soaring flight,
In chaos, we find our might.

Whirlwinds of passion, fierce and raw,
The rush ignites what we saw.
Bound by ties, we draw the straw,
In frenzy's grip, we find our law.

Rhapsody in Turmoil

Melodies rise from chaos deep,
Notes that weave through thoughts we keep.
In turmoil, a promise to leap,
A rhapsody for hearts to weep.

Harmony lost, yet still we sing,
Chasing shadows that pain may bring.
Through the storm, our voices ring,
A joyful sound, on hope's wing.

Dichotomy of Desire

Yearning pulls at heart and soul,
A dance between the whole and a hole.
In every spark, we lose control,
Desires clash, we pay the toll.

Paths diverge in passion's realm,
With every wave, we grief overwhelm.
In shadows cast, we're at the helm,
Navigating where wishes overwhelm.

The Eye of the Storm

In the center calm lays wide,
Whispers of winds collide.
Nature's fury rages loud,
Yet here I stand, unbowed.

Turbulence dances around,
With silence in this ground.
Storm clouds swirl in dark delight,
But peace hovers, holding tight.

Lightning flashes, shadows play,
A paradox in disarray.
In chaos, wisdom finds a way,
Here I linger, come what may.

The storm will pass, as storms do go,
But lessons learned will ever grow.
For in the eye, there's strength untold,
In heart of tempest, I feel bold.

Cacophony of Emotions

Raging waves crash in my chest,
A symphony, it knows no rest.
Fury, joy, sadness collide,
A clash I cannot hide.

Voices whisper, scream, and wail,
In this tempest, I set sail.
Fragile hearts explode and mend,
Somber journeys with no end.

A canvas splashed with colors bright,
Each brushstroke, a memory's flight.
In shadows, laughter finds a way,
In silence, words have much to say.

Through this discord, I shall seek,
The harmony beneath the peak.
In chaos, find the song I need,
To plant the calm, to sow the seed.

Silhouettes of Ecstasy

Midnight dances bathed in light,
Figures sway, lost in night.
Pulse of music, heartbeats race,
In shadows, pure love I trace.

Starlit kisses, fleeting dreams,
In twilight, nothing's as it seems.
Bodies move with rhythm divine,
Whispers soft, the world is mine.

Each glance ignites a burning spark,
In the dark, I leave my mark.
Together, we fade and flow,
In this bliss, time ceases to go.

Silhouettes in the moonlight gleam,
Living, loving, as if a dream.
In every laugh, in every sigh,
In ecstasy, we learn to fly.

Rains of Reflection

Raindrops fall like whispered thoughts,
Cascading down, they tie the knots.
Every teardrop tells a tale,
In puddles deep, dreams unveil.

Clouds above begin to cry,
Echoes linger in the sky.
In nature's tears, I find my peace,
A quiet moment where worries cease.

Mirrors form on sidewalks bright,
Reflecting hopes, a fleeting light.
In each drop, a story swells,
Secrets held in nature's wells.

When the storm begins to fade,
In stillness, solace is laid.
The rains of reflection cleanse the soul,
In each storm, we find our whole.

Celestial Tug-of-War

Stars collide in silent night,
Galaxies twist in cosmic light.
Gravity pulls with unseen hands,
While dreams dance on stardust strands.

Moon whispers secrets to the sky,
While comets race as they fly by.
Time sways gently, never still,
In this duel of fate and will.

Planets spin in their own grace,
Each a story, each a place.
In the dark, the struggle grows,
As the universe pulses and flows.

Black holes hunger, light bends near,
Across the void, we drift and steer.
A tug-of-war without an end,
In the vastness where we transcend.

Maelstrom of the Mind

Thoughts swirl like leaves in wind,
A chaotic dance that won't rescind.
Ideas clash, a fierce embrace,
In the whirlpool, I find my place.

Memories flicker, shadows play,
In the storm, they twist and sway.
Logic drowns in the waves of fear,
Yet in the chaos, I find what's dear.

Voices echo, whispers loud,
Beneath the surface, emotions crowd.
A tempest brews in silent cries,
As reason battles and slowly dies.

In the eddies, clarity hides,
A fragile peace where chaos abides.
Through the storm, I seek to find,
A tranquil sea within my mind.

Tempest of Emotions

Waves crash hard against the shore,
Emotions rise, they ebb and pour.
Joy and sorrow, tangled together,
A storm brews strong in any weather.

Lightning strikes in flashes bright,
Passion ignites and takes to flight.
Love can soar, but also fall,
In the tempest, we rise and stall.

Raging winds of doubt and fear,
Whisper low, and draw us near.
Hope glimmers through the raging heat,
A lighthouse guiding through my defeat.

In the aftermath, the calm draws near,
A quiet voice that I can hear.
From the depths, I rise anew,
In the tempest, I find what's true.

Storms Within the Heart

Thunder rumbles deep inside,
A tempest that I cannot hide.
Each heartbeat echoes like the rain,
A constant rhythm laced with pain.

In the shadows, feelings swell,
A silent war where silence dwells.
Tears like raindrops fall and blend,
In the storm, I seek to mend.

Love's sweet whisper, then the roar,
Passion's tide crashes on the floor.
Hope and sorrow weave a thread,
In the fabric of the words unsaid.

Yet from this storm, new light will break,
In the turmoil, strength I make.
As winds settle, peace will start,
To calm the storms within my heart.

Fractured Sunshine

Sunlight spills through broken glass,
Fragile beams play upon the grass.
Each shard reflects a tale untold,
In fleeting moments, life unfolds.

Whispers of warmth in shadows cast,
The past is gone, but memories last.
Glimmers dance in the evening breeze,
Fractured dreams bring hearts to ease.

A Flurry of Yearning

Snowflakes drift in the pale moon's glow,
Softly falling, like hopes we sow.
Each flake alive, a wish in flight,
Painting the world in silvery light.

A longing stirs beneath the frost,
For warmth of love that feels like loss.
In the quiet night, hearts expand,
In the flurry, we make our stand.

Tornado of Desire

Whirling winds with a fierce embrace,
A tempest brews in this wild space.
Passion and chaos, a dance so grand,
In the vortex, we understand.

Yearning hearts caught in the spin,
Lost in the storm, we can't begin.
Yet in the chaos, we find our way,
Through the desire that holds sway.

The Whirl of Longing

Leaves turn in a gentle twirl,
A cycle of hope, like a dancer's whirl.
Each rustle sings of dreams we chase,
In the autumn's breath, we find our place.

Time flows swift, like a river's song,
In every current, we feel we belong.
The whirl of longing weaves us tight,
In the tapestry of day and night.

Dance of the Inner Tempest

In shadows deep, the fight begins,
A swirling storm, where silence spins.
Heartbeats clash like thunder loud,
Within this tempest, lost, unbowed.

Waves of doubt crash on the shore,
Memories rise, then fade once more.
In twilight's grasp, I feel the pull,
A dance of fire, fierce and full.

Breath of winds, a whispered plea,
Carry me forth, set this heart free.
The rhythm sways, a haunting song,
In chaos found, where I belong.

Through raging seas, I find my path,
Embracing storm, I face its wrath.
With every turn, I learn to glide,
In the tempest's arms, my truth won't hide.

Veil of Mixed Signals

In the silence, words unspoken,
Promises drift, easily broken.
Eyes meet hearts in fleeting chance,
Lost in the web of a half-hearted dance.

Colors blend in a fractured light,
Day turns to dusk, from wrong to right.
Signals cross in a twisted fate,
Caught in the limbo of love and hate.

Fingers reach for truth concealed,
But masks remain, the wounds, unhealed.
Each glance a question, a hesitant sigh,
Under the veil, we silently lie.

Yet in the chaos, a spark ignites,
Hope flutters softly in quiet nights.
Through the shroud, we'll find our way,
In mixed signals, a brand new day.

Mirage of Serenity

In the distance, calm waters gleam,
A vision caught within a dream.
Whispers of peace, so sweetly call,
Yet closer, I find the shadows fall.

The sunlit shore, a deceptive guise,
Reflections charm with painted lies.
As I step forth, the waves retreat,
A fleeting calm, a bitter sweet.

Silence sings through cypress trees,
A lullaby kissed by the breeze.
But beneath the surface, storms arise,
In the mirage, truth often hides.

Searching for stillness, my heart does roam,
In waves of doubt, I seek a home.
Yet every step brings clarity near,
In the struggle, I learn to hear.

Whistles of the Unknown

Through misty paths, a whistle calls,
Inviting wanderers, as twilight falls.
The echoes resonate in night's embrace,
A journey awaits, in shadowed space.

Footsteps guide through the thickened air,
Each note a promise, a silent dare.
The eerie tune, both near and far,
Pulls me deeper, beneath a star.

Secrets linger in the night's deep fold,
Stories whisper where the brave are bold.
With every breeze, a chance is thrown,
With every whistle, a truth is sown.

To the unknown, I'm drawn like flame,
In this symphony, I find my name.
Embrace the echoes, let the heart roam,
In the whistling night, I am home.

The Dance of Shadows

In twilight's grip, we twirl and sway,
Through whispers dark, they weave their play.
A silhouette in the moonglow bright,
We lose ourselves in the veil of night.

Echoes of laughter, a haunting song,
The shadows stretch, where we belong.
With every step, a tale unfolds,
In the dance of shadows, our story told.

They flicker close, then drift away,
In the silent hush, our hearts relay.
A rhythm beats where fears reside,
In shadows' embrace, we don't need to hide.

So let us dance till the break of dawn,
In shades of grey, we are reborn.
With every twirl, let us ignite,
The dance of shadows in the night.

Labyrinthine Emotions

Winding paths through minds we roam,
In each corner, we seek a home.
Twists and turns of heart's design,
In the maze of feelings, we intertwine.

A flicker of hope, then clouds of despair,
Searching for solace, gasping for air.
In the silence deep, we confront our fights,
Finding our way through the endless nights.

Every choice a fork in the road,
Wounds and stories, a heavy load.
Yet, in chaos, we find our peace,
In labyrinthine emotions, we seek release.

With courage bold, we face the storm,
In the heart's labyrinth, we learn to transform.
Through winding roads, we must confront,
The beauty hidden in the emotional hunt.

A Choreography of Confusion

In the tangle of thoughts, we find our feet,
Steps misaligned, yet bittersweet.
A rhythm lost upon the ground,
In confusion's grasp, we're tightly bound.

Each gesture speaks what words cannot,
In silent screams, the battles fought.
Through missteps large, we seek the grace,
In this wild dance, we embrace the pace.

Twirling thoughts like autumn leaves,
A canvas blurred, yet hope believes.
In every stumble, a new refrain,
A choreography born from pain.

So let's sway to the music of the mind,
In the chaos of hearts, solace we find.
Together we dance, lost but free,
In the confusion, just you and me.

Waves of Conflicted Dreams

The ocean stirs with restless tides,
In dreams we chase, where hope abides.
Waves crash hard against the shore,
Each conflict whispers, imploring more.

The sunlight glints on waters deep,
In every wave, a promise to keep.
Yet shadows linger in the foam,
In dreams we build, we seek a home.

Tidal forces, pulling with might,
Our hearts collide in the moon's sweet light.
Amidst the chaos, we find our way,
In each wave's crest, a brand new day.

So ride the swells of what we feel,
In waves of dreams, our truths reveal.
Through every storm, we'll learn to swim,
In the ocean's embrace, our spirits brim.

Seasons of Unrest

In winter's chill, we find our fears,
The quiet whispers of lost years.
Spring brings hope, but storms soon rise,
A clash of tempests fills the skies.

Summer fades, and shadows creep,
In autumn's twilight, secrets keep.
The cycle turns, but pain remains,
Through every season, heartache reigns.

Whirl of Joy and Sorrow

In laughter's dance, we lose our breath,
Yet, shadows linger, hinting death.
Joy spins round, like leaves in flight,
But sorrow waits, both day and night.

A carousel of day and night,
Where smiles meet tears in soft twilight.
We twirl through moments sweet and bitter,
In every heart, a hidden glitter.

Rift of Passion

Two hearts collide, a blazing fire,
Each touch ignites a fierce desire.
Yet in the heat, a crack appears,
A fragile bond, it's riddled with fears.

The pull of love, a tightrope walk,
Words unspoken, the silence talks.
In passion's grip, the rift grows wide,
An endless battle we can't abide.

The Upside-Down Heart

A heart that beats with colors bright,
Is often lost in darkest night.
It flips and flops, then turns to stone,
In love's embrace, we're all alone.

Yet through the chaos, hope does rise,
Each scar a tale, beneath the skies.
With every beat, we learn to cope,
An upside-down heart seeks for hope.

Dance of Turbulent Thoughts

In shadows deep, they swirl and sway,
A tempest formed, come what may.
Chasing dreams, lost in the fray,
Whispers dance, then fade away.

A twirl of hopes, a flash of fear,
Each step unsteady, drawing near.
In chaos' grip, the mind will steer,
A silent scream, a cry sincere.

Between the beats, a pause to breathe,
The heart contends, yet dreams believe.
Ensnared in thoughts, we sometimes weave,
In reckless time, we gently cleave.

Yet through the storm, a light does gleam,
A flicker born from fragile dream.
In turbulent sway, we find the seam,
And dance once more, a flowing stream.

Chaos of the Soul

In echoes loud, the spirits fight,
A battle rages, day and night.
Between the dark and beams of light,
The chaos brews, a daunting sight.

A tempest tossed within the chest,
Where questions linger, never rest.
A heart that aches, a soul distressed,
In every glance, a silent quest.

Yet in the wild, a whisper calls,
From broken dreams, the spirit sprawls.
With every rise, the shadow falls,
In chaos, truth softly enthralls.

Through tangled paths, we seek the way,
Embracing night as much as day.
Our souls entwined, come what may,
In chaos found, we learn to sway.

Cyclone of Remorse

A whirlwind stirs within the heart,
Regrets assemble, tearing apart.
Each choice a thorn, a furious dart,
In silence deep, we play our part.

The winds of time, a cruel embrace,
Stride through shadows, lost in space.
The haunting ghosts we cannot face,
In swirling thought, we find our place.

Yet through the storm of what has passed,
A glimmer shines, a hope amassed.
With every breath, the die is cast,
And in the cyclone, free at last.

Amidst the chaos, healing breaks,
In whispered winds, the heart remakes.
With every turn, our spirit wakes,
In cyclone's core, the soul creates.

Tidal Waves of Euphoria

Upon the shore where dreams collide,
The waves of joy come in with pride.
In bursts of laughter, we confide,
With every crest, we swell inside.

A rhythm danced in pure delight,
The sun-kissed moments shine so bright.
In hearts alive, we chase the height,
As euphoria takes its flight.

In crashing tides, we lose our fears,
The sound of joy, the echo cheers.
In liquid dreams, we drown our tears,
As waves of bliss draw us near.

So let them roll, these waves so grand,
With open hearts, we take the stand.
In tide and time, we'll make our brand,
And ride the joy, forever planned.

Raging River of Dreams

In the night, the river flows,
Carrying whispers, tales of woe.
Stars above, a distant gleam,
Guiding hearts through a troubled dream.

Rushing waters, fierce and wild,
Hold the secrets of every child.
Fears and hopes in currents blend,
Journeying forth, no start or end.

Listen close to the water's song,
A melody sweet, where we belong.
Underneath the surface deep,
Lies the promise we dare to keep.

As we sail on this vast stream,
Trust in fate, in love, in dream.
For in the flow, we find our way,
Through raging nights and brightening day.

Echoes of Turmoil

Whispers linger in the air,
Tales of loss, of deep despair.
Voices rise from shadows past,
Echoing sorrows, shadows cast.

In the silence, tension grows,
Every heartbeat, turmoil flows.
Waves of fear crash at the shore,
Inviting thoughts we can't ignore.

Yet in chaos, strength is found,
Beneath the storm, on lifted ground.
From turmoil's ashes, we arise,
Glimmers of hope in tearful skies.

Hear the echoes, let them guide,
Through the tempest, stand with pride.
For every struggle, every fight,
Leads to dawn and newfound light.

Hurricane of Hope

In the midst of winds so fierce,
Hope emerges, hearts it pierce.
Through the gales, a voice so clear,
Calls us forth, to persevere.

Though the skies are dark with dread,
Seeds of courage, softly spread.
In the tempest, dreams take flight,
Navigating through the night.

Winds may howl and rain may fall,
But hope endures, it binds us all.
In the chaos, find the calm,
A gentle force, a healing balm.

As the storm begins to wane,
Hope will shine through all the pain.
With every breath, let spirits rise,
A hurricane of brighter skies.

Whispers in the Maelstrom

In the heart of the swirling sea,
Whispers call, beckon to me.
Voices soft, a soothing rhyme,
Guiding lost souls through the clime.

Amidst the whirl, uncertainty reigns,
Yet in the chaos, love remains.
Waves may crash, and shadows creep,
But in the depths, we trust and leap.

Every moment, every breath,
In the maelstrom, we find depth.
Fragile threads of hope entwined,
Lean into the truth we've signed.

For in the storm, we shall find grace,
In whispers soft, a warm embrace.
Embrace the chaos, dance along,
For in the maelstrom, we are strong.

Twisting Paths of Yearning

Beneath the stars, my heart does roam,
In shadows deep, I search for home.
With every turn, the whispers call,
A longing heart, it craves it all.

Through winding trails where dreams collide,
I chase the echoes, nowhere to hide.
Each step I take, the night unfolds,
The story of a heart that molds.

In silence found, the world retreats,
Yet in this stillness, longing beats.
A compass spun by fate's own hand,
To guide my soul through shifting sand.

Unbridled Tempers

In raging storms, the tempers flare,
With thunder loud, we strip our care.
Words like lightning pull apart,
Yet passion fuels the raging heart.

With fierceness born from heated fights,
We clash like titans in darkest nights.
But in the gale, a truth is found,
In chaos lies a bond profound.

With every word, we break and mend,
A cycle spun that knows no end.
In fire's dance, we dare to roam,
Untamed, we find our way back home.

Cascade of Sentiments

A river flows with whispers sweet,
Each drop a memory, love's heartbeat.
In gentle currents, feelings rise,
A tapestry of worlds and skies.

Like petals fall in soft embrace,
The moments linger, time, a trace.
With every wave, emotions swell,
In quiet ripples, stories tell.

Through sunlight bright, or shadows cast,
The cascade flows, a song to last.
With every glance, a world anew,
In every drop, it's me and you.

Raging Fire Within

A flame ignites beneath the skin,
With passion fierce, it draws me in.
Each flicker holds a secret tight,
A burning wish within the night.

In whispered doubts, the embers glow,
Through trials faced, the fire will grow.
Despite the storms, it finds a way,
To blaze anew with each new day.

In depths of heart, where shadows play,
The raging fire won't fade away.
I'll stoke the flame, embrace the heat,
For in this blaze, I feel complete.

The Turbulent Sea of Thought

Waves crash against the shore,
Thoughts swirl like tempest tides.
Ideas collide with fervor,
In chaos, clarity hides.

Sailing ships of reason lost,
Navigating through the storm.
Each crest a fleeting moment,
To which new truths can be born.

In the depths, shadows linger,
Where whispers of doubt reside.
Yet, amidst the howling winds,
Hope breaks through, a fleeting guide.

The sea calms, a gentle breath,
Thoughts drift like clouds at dusk.
Finding peace in the silence,
In stillness, the mind can trust.

Eclipsed by Emotion

A shadow falls on sunlight,
When feelings take their toll.
Like an eclipse, they cover,
The heart's deep and aching whole.

Joy flickers like a candle,
Dimmed by clouds of despair.
Moments pass in silence,
Lost in heavy, stagnant air.

Yet, the light returns at dawn,
Colors burst like blooms anew.
Emotion shifts like seasons,
Into skies of brilliant blue.

In the dance of light and dark,
A balance starts to form.
Emotions may eclipse the heart,
But love can keep it warm.

Balance on the Edge

Between reason and emotion,
I walk a fragile line.
The whispers call to wobble,
Yet I seek to redefine.

It's a dance of give and take,
As I sway with every breath.
Finding strength in shaky moments,
Life's beauty lives in depth.

Each step holds uncertainty,
A choice between the two.
But in the midst of chaos,
I find my path is true.

With courage as my anchor,
I embrace the blessèd sway.
On this edge of life I balance,
In harmony, I stay.

Veils of Distortion

Behind the glass, a vision sways,
Reality bends and distorts.
Veils of perception cloud my eyes,
And truth becomes a fleeting thought.

Mirrored fragments scatter light,
Revealing only parts of me.
Each mask I wear, a piece of self,
In shadows, I long to be free.

But through the haze, a whisper calls,
An echo of what lies within.
The layers start to peel away,
To reveal where I begin.

With every veil I lift and part,
A deeper sight unfurls.
In the dance of distortion,
I find the light of worlds.

Flurries of Affection

In a gentle breeze we sway,
Hearts entwined in soft display.
Echoes of laughter in the air,
Whispers of love, so pure, so rare.

Snowflakes dance in twilight's glow,
Moments shared, a sweet tableau.
Each glance, a spark, ignites the night,
In flurries warm, our hearts take flight.

Beneath the stars, the world fades away,
In your arms, I long to stay.
What magic wraps this tender bliss,
In every touch, a fleeting kiss.

Together we weave through winter's embrace,
Finding warmth in a cold, vast space.
As flurries kiss the ground beneath,
Our love blooms bright, an endless wreath.

Shadows in the Gale

Whispers lost in the swirling breeze,
Underneath the ancient trees.
Shadows flicker, dance and play,
In the quiet night, they fade away.

Moonlight casts its silver beams,
Filling the sky with fragile dreams.
A chill runs deep through hollowed halls,
As the night softly calls.

Voices echo through the dark,
Every rustle, an untamed spark.
Caught between the light and shade,
In fleeting moments, memories fade.

Yet in the tempest, truth prevails,
As we navigate these shadowed trails.
Love persists through wind and rain,
In the kaleidoscope of joy and pain.

Rapture's Wild Flight

Through skies of blue, our spirits soar,
Where dreams take wing, and hearts explore.
Each pulse, a rhythm, a daring quest,
In rapture's wild flight, we find our rest.

Clouds whisper secrets, bold and free,
Every moment, a new decree.
With every breeze, our souls ignite,
Boundless passion in the night.

The world beneath is but a blur,
As we chase the winds that stir.
Above the chaos, we find a way,
In rapture's hold, we shall not sway.

Together we dance on the edge of time,
In perfect harmony, our hearts in rhyme.
Let the stars guide us through the night,
On rapture's wings, we take our flight.

Whirl of Unspoken Words

In a space where silence sings,
Thoughts entwined, the heart takes wings.
A glance exchanged, electric spark,
In this moment, we leave our mark.

Words unspoken, yet understood,
Every heartbeat, a promise good.
In the stillness, emotions swirl,
Love's soft whisper, a tender pearl.

Around us, time begins to bend,
In the quiet, we find a friend.
A dance of light, a fleeting glance,
In gentle waves, we take our chance.

The world outside is far away,
In this whirl, we choose to stay.
With every breath, our hearts embark,
In the beauty of this silent arc.

Fractured Whispers

In shadows deep where secrets dwell,
Fractured whispers weave their spell.
Echoes linger, soft and light,
Carried softly through the night.

Shattered dreams on whispered breath,
Tales of love, and hints of death.
In the stillness, voices call,
A murmur rising, a gentle fall.

Each word a thread, a fragile lace,
Holding time in a tender embrace.
Through broken silence, hearts align,
In fractured whispers, souls entwine.

Like autumn leaves on swirling air,
They dance with joy, they ache with care.
In the silence, truths unfold,
Fractured whispers, stories told.

Gale of Memory

A whirlwind spins through fading light,
Memories swirl, day into night.
In the gale, lost tales arise,
Carried forth beneath the skies.

A laughter shared, a lingering sigh,
In gentle moments, we sometimes cry.
Through stormy paths, we chase the past,
In the gale of memory, shadows cast.

With every gust, a piece takes flight,
Shattering calm, igniting the night.
Echoes of joy, whispers of pain,
In the gale of memory, hearts remain.

As time doth fade, horizons blend,
In every gust, a chance to mend.
Through every storm, we learn to see,
The gale of memory sets us free.

Tidal Waves of Emotion

Beneath the surface, currents sway,
Tidal waves of emotion play.
Crashing hearts, the ebb and flow,
In every undertow, feelings grow.

The rise and fall, a steady beat,
In swirling tides, our souls meet.
Rising peaks of joy and pain,
Tidal waves wash over again.

In stormy seas, we learn to dive,
For love and loss, we strive to survive.
With every wave, we're pulled apart,
Yet find the strength in every heart.

From depths unknown, we find our way,
Drifting softly with the spray.
In ocean's dance and subtle grace,
Tidal waves of emotion embrace.

Spiral of Heartstrings

In a world spun with threads unseen,
A spiral of heartstrings weaves between.
Ties that bind, both strong and frail,
In love's embrace, we set our sail.

Woven gently, each moment caught,
In every glance, a lesson taught.
Through laughter's glow and sorrow's sting,
In the spiral, our hearts take wing.

Each twist a story, each turn a chance,
In life's great dance, we find romance.
With every heartbeat, connections grow,
In the spiral of heartstrings, we flow.

As seasons change, and time moves on,
The spiral tightens, then we're gone.
Yet love remains, an endless thread,
In the spiral of heartstrings, we are led.

Cyclone of Longing

In the heart, a tempest grows,
Waves of yearning, ebb and flow.
Whispers call from distant shores,
Echoes of love, forever more.

Each moment stretches, time stands still,
Chasing shadows, against my will.
Fingers grasp at empty air,
With each breath, the world lays bare.

Dreams take flight on winds of fate,
Lost in silence, love's weight abates.
The eye reveals a tranquil place,
Yet longing burns, a fierce embrace.

When the storm has blown away,
Will I find you, come what may?
In the calm, my heart beats loud,
Cyclone still, beneath the cloud.

Tornado of Thoughts

Spiraling whispers twist and shake,
Thoughts collide, a fierce earthquake.
Images flash, a blinding light,
Fleeting dreams take off in flight.

Voices merge, then fade away,
Time turns fast, then goes astray.
In the chaos, clarity seeks,
Truths emerge from tangled peaks.

A whirlwind spins through the night,
Searching for a single light.
Ideas clash, then gently blend,
In the storm, my heart transcends.

As silence falls, what's left but grace?
The tornado leaves its trace.
From the wreckage, hope will grow,
Thoughts transformed, like seeds will sow.

Torn Veil of Desire

A veil hangs, tattered and thin,
Behind it lies the dance within.
Fingers brush against the seam,
In the shadows, lovers dream.

Whispers soft, like falling leaves,
Stir the heart and soul believes.
Yearning pulls with gentle strength,
Desire stretches at full length.

Time stands still, while passions flare,
In this space, we are laid bare.
Beneath the veil, the truth is spun,
In the dark, we become one.

When the dawn breaks light anew,
Will the veil reveal our hue?
With tender hands, we mend the fray,
In the light, our wishes sway.

Whims of the Storm

Nature's breath, a capricious sigh,
Storm clouds gather, gray the sky.
Raindrops dance on window panes,
While thunder rumbles, love remains.

Each gust carries a story told,
Of hearts entwined, both brave and bold.
Lightning strikes, a moment's thrill,
In chaos, quiet hearts stand still.

The winds may howl, but we embrace,
With every pulse, we find our place.
Whims of storms shape paths we tread,
Where truths collide and dreams are bred.

As the tempest fades to calm,
We discover peace, a healing balm.
In the aftermath, we will find,
A love that lingers, intertwined.

Tempest of the Heart

Winds of sorrow, howling low,
Clouds of doubt, they come and go.
Thunder rumbles in the night,
Lightning flashes, a jarring light.

Fury rises, waves of pain,
In this storm, I feel the strain.
Yet in chaos, hope takes hold,
A silver lining, bright and bold.

Raindrops fall; the heart beats fast,
In the tempest, I am cast.
But as the storm begins to wane,
Peace emerges after pain.

From the ashes, I will rise,
With the dawn, I'll claim my skies.
The tempest rages, yet I find,
Strength and grace, intertwined.

Swirling Echoes

In the silence, whispers call,
Soft reflections, memories fall.
The echoes dance, they twist and twine,
A haunting song, both dark and fine.

Through the corridors of the mind,
Lost in shadows, truth confined.
Yet in the folds of time, I see,
Fragments of what used to be.

Swirling tales of joy and woe,
In the heart, they ebb and flow.
Each echo whispers time's embrace,
Fading gently, leaving lace.

A symphony of thought and dream,
In every note, a silent scream.
The swirling echoes, I must face,
Unraveling in this sacred space.

Chaotic Emotions Unleashed

Raging tides of joy and grief,
In this chaos, I find relief.
A tempest brewing deep inside,
Wild and free, I cannot hide.

Colors clash within my soul,
Churning feelings take their toll.
Laughter mixes with despair,
A whirlwind's pull, a frantic scare.

Anger spills, a fierce outcry,
A desperate urge to touch the sky.
Yet amidst the roar, a gentle sigh,
Balancing storms that rise and die.

In the chaos, truth appears,
Every scream, reflected tears.
Emotions raw, they spring to life,
A dance of passion, love, and strife.

Dance of the Unraveled Soul

Twisting gently, freely spun,
In the moonlight, I am one.
With each movement, threads unwind,
The fabric of the heart, unconfined.

Footfalls whisper on the ground,
With every beat, I am unbound.
A tapestry of hopes and dreams,
In every waltz, my spirit gleams.

Flickers of joy, embers of pain,
In this dance, there's much to gain.
With every leap, I find my way,
The unraveled soul, in full display.

As the music swells, I rise,
With the rhythm, touch the skies.
A dance of life, both brave and true,
In this freedom, I find you.

Blustery Skies of the Mind

Thoughts like clouds that twist and sway,
In winds of doubt, they drift away.
A storm brews strong, a flash of light,
In blustery skies, I search for flight.

Waves of chaos crash and roar,
Whispers fading from the shore.
In swirling tempests, I find peace,
A calm within, my doubts release.

Raindrops tap like gentle keys,
Unlocking truths from hidden leaves.
A rainbow forms when storms subside,
In blustery skies, I find my guide.

As dusk descends, the winds grow mild,
The mind reclaims its silent child.
With every gust, I learn to see,
The beauty in this vast esprit.

Echoing Vortex

In the depths of silence, sounds collide,
A swirling vortex, where echoes hide.
Memories spiral, dancing free,
In the hush of night, they call to me.

Whispers linger, softly spun,
Ghostly traces of laughter run.
Through the dark, their shadows weave,
In echoing dreams, we believe.

Time cascades in endless loops,
Each note unfolds, like ancient troops.
A symphony of shadows vast,
In this vortex, I'm embraced at last.

As tones entwine, the world ignites,
Fleeting moments, glowing lights.
In the echo, I find my face,
Reflected back in time and space.

Fluttering Heartstrings

In the stillness, whispers follow,
Gentle breezes, soft and hollow.
Heartstrings pull like tender ties,
Fluttering secrets beneath the skies.

A sparrow sings of love's sweet chase,
In every note, I find my place.
Threads of hope weave through the night,
In fluttering dreams, I take my flight.

With every beat, the shadows dance,
In fleeting glances, lost romance.
Moments shimmer like fireflies,
In the twilight, where feeling lies.

As dawn awakes and colors blend,
The heartstrings stretch, but never bend.
In fluttering rhythms, I will grow,
Through every heart, the love will flow.

Celestial Confusion

Stars whisper secrets in the dark,
Galaxies spinning, each a spark.
In the vastness of the night,
Celestial confusion takes its flight.

Constellations twist and fade,
Stories told, yet they evade.
Lost in dreams of cosmic rhyme,
In heavenly chaos, I find my time.

Planets clash in silent screams,
Echoes trapped in cosmic beams.
Through the fog, I seek the light,
In celestial hopes, I take my flight.

As dawn approaches, heavens sigh,
Wiping tears from the painted sky.
In the confusion, clarity gleams,
A universe spun from vibrant dreams.

The Pulse of Dissonance

In shadows cast by whispered fears,
A rhythm beats that no one hears.
The clash of dreams, a haunting song,
Where right feels wrong, and wrong feels strong.

Silent screams in muted nights,
Dissonance of fading lights.
Hearts that tremble, minds that break,
Each pulse a choice, each choice a stake.

Lost in echoes of despair,
A dance of sorrow, none to share.
Yet in the chaos, sparks ignite,
For from the dark, emerges light.

So let the pulse of discord play,
And chase the shadows far away.
For harmony may rise anew,
From all the trials we once knew.

The Echo of Unseen Storms

Whispers travel on the breeze,
Carrying tales from distant seas.
Clouds gather in the twilight sky,
Unseen storms that loom nearby.

With every gust, a secret sigh,
Unfolding dreams that dare to fly.
The world prepares for nature's might,
As shadows dance with creeping fright.

Lightning flickers, thunder roars,
A symphony on hidden shores.
Yet in the depths, a calm prevails,
As echoes weave through whispered tales.

In quiet moments, storms are born,
Unraveled thus, the night is torn.
Yet from the chaos, life shall spring,
In every storm, a song to sing.

In the Eye of Emotion

Within the storm, a stillness grows,
In swirling winds, a bloom bestows.
Amidst the chaos, a heart beats true,
In the eye's embrace, a world anew.

Tides of passion, ebb and flow,
Surging waves and undertow.
In every tear that falls like rain,
A whispered joy, a touch of pain.

Moments linger, tender, raw,
Held within a silent law.
In fleeting glances, lives collide,
In the eye of emotion, souls abide.

So let us dance in the eye's grace,
Where love and fear both find their place.
For in this stillness, life expands,
In the heart's depths, we take our stands.

Threads of Rapture

Weaving dreams in colors bright,
Threads of rapture, pure delight.
Each moment stitched with love and care,
In the tapestry, we dare to share.

Silk and linen, soft and bold,
Stories woven, secrets told.
With every knot, a bond takes flight,
Frayed edges glow in the fading light.

Capturing laughter, catching tears,
Stitching together all our fears.
In patterns rich, our lives entwine,
In every seam, a sign divine.

So let us gather every thread,
In the fabric where we are led.
For in this weave, we find our way,
Threads of rapture, brightening the day.

Serenade of Mixed Sentiments

In twilight's glow, our shadows dance,
Whispered hopes in fleeting chance.
A tender touch, a bitter sigh,
In love's embrace, we learn to fly.

Yet storms may brew within the heart,
As passion's fire may tear apart.
A laughter shared, a silent pain,
In joy's sweet song, we hide the strain.

With every note, our spirits blend,
A serenade that will not end.
Through joy and sorrow, we'll remain,
In mixed sentiments, love will reign.

So hand in hand, we'll chart the stars,
A tapestry of wounds and scars.
In every heartbeat, truth unfolds,
Our serenade, forever holds.

Unraveling Threads of Yearning

In the quiet hour before the dawn,
A web of dreams is delicately drawn.
Threads of longing, woven tight,
Catch the whispers of the night.

Each string a story, layered deep,
Of promises made, and secrets to keep.
The heart's own map, a woven desire,
Unraveling slowly, setting hearts afire.

With every tug, a question lingers,
What fate awaits in life's vast fingers?
As moments stitch the past to now,
In this tapestry, we all do vow.

To seek the light in shadow's veil,
To listen close, to know, to sail.
Unraveling threads that bind us here,
In yearning's charm, we conquer fear.

Vortex of Hidden Truths

In swirling depths where shadows play,
Secrets linger, lost in gray.
A vortex spins, both fierce and slow,
Revealing tales of joy and woe.

Each truth a star, obscured by night,
In the chaos, we search for light.
What lies beneath the surface calm?
A tempest wild, or fleeting balm?

Yet wisdom blooms in cracks of pain,
A quiet voice, our hearts remain.
Through storms of doubt, we journey wide,
In the vortex, truth cannot hide.

In every swirl, a lesson learned,
Through hidden truths, our spirits turned.
In the dance of fate, we find our way,
Embracing all, come what may.

The Sway of Unshed Tears

In twilight's hush, emotions swell,
A tender tale, we know too well.
The weight of words left unexpressed,
Within the heart, a quiet quest.

Each tear unshed, a story's woe,
A river deep that yearns to flow.
The smile we wear, a fragile mask,
In silence held, we dare to ask.

Yet softly bends the willow tree,
In sorrow's grace, we find the key.
For every drop that falls unseen,
Brings forth the strength to heal, to dream.

In time's embrace, the hurt will fade,
And from the dark, new paths are laid.
In the sway of unshed tears, we grow,
In each sweet sorrow, love will show.

Cascade of Conflicts

Rivers of anger swell and rise,
Whispers of doubt beneath the skies.
In the rush, we lose our way,
Caught in the fray of yesterday.

Voices clash, the echoes scream,
Chasing shadows, lost in a dream.
Each turn a test, each choice a fight,
Navigating wrongs to find the right.

Rocks of despair beneath our feet,
A journey marked by bitter heat.
Yet in the turmoil, hope ignites,
Guiding souls through darkest nights.

Through the roar, a whisper calls,
In the chaos, love never falls.
Amidst the conflict, we will stand,
With open hearts, united hand in hand.

Tempestuous Nights

Winds howl loudly, skies turn grey,
Hearts beat wildly, led astray.
Each flash of lightning, a spark of fear,
In the turmoil, dreams appear.

Raindrops dance on window panes,
Echoes linger as hope wanes.
Yet through shadows, starlight gleams,
Guiding us to brighter dreams.

Whispers drown in the thunder's roar,
Yet love's embrace we still explore.
With every storm, our spirits rise,
Finding solace beneath dark skies.

When dawn breaks, the colors bloom,
Chasing away the night's cold gloom.
In every tempest, we find our song,
Together, where we truly belong.

Symphony of Uncertainty

Notes of doubt, a discorded start,
Each measure pulls at the heart.
In the silence, questions weave,
A tapestry of what we believe.

Lost in rhythms of the unknown,
The melody of life has grown.
A dance of chance, a fleeting beat,
In every stumble, we find our feet.

Echoes linger, time moves slow,
In the dissonance, seeds we sow.
Harmony waits just out of sight,
Guiding us through the enveloping night.

With each note, the journey unfolds,
In uncertainty, the future holds.
Together we face the grand unknown,
In this symphony, we are never alone.

Labyrinth of Emotion

Twists and turns within the mind,
Each corner hides what we may find.
Fear and joy dance side by side,
In this maze, our hearts reside.

Walls of memory trap the past,
A fleeting moment that could not last.
Yet every path leads to a choice,
In every silence, we hear our voice.

Through the shadows, light can seep,
In the labyrinth, secrets keep.
An inner journey, complex and wild,
Awakening the heart of a child.

Finding the way, piece by piece,
Amidst the chaos, seek release.
In this maze of emotion, we strive,
To uncover the truth that keeps us alive.

Chasing the Storm

Dark clouds gather, thunder calls,
Lightning splits, the silence falls.
Winds whip wild, they dance and soar,
I chase the storm, forevermore.

Raindrops fall like silver tears,
Washing away my deepest fears.
Nature's roar, a fierce delight,
I run to meet the stormy night.

In the chaos, I find my place,
Heart racing in this wild embrace.
A symphony of wind and rain,
Chasing the storm, I feel no pain.

With every flash, a spark ignites,
In the darkness, the heart takes flight.
The tempest sings, a haunting tune,
As I dance beneath the moon.

Whispers in the Whirlwind

Softly spoken, secrets glide,
Through the chaos, they confide.
Whispers dance on gusty air,
In the whirlwind, dreams laid bare.

Echoes flutter, fragile sounds,
In the tempest, hope abounds.
The unseen, a gentle touch,
In the storm, it means so much.

Thoughts like leaves, swirling free,
Carried far, across the sea.
In their flight, a story told,
Whispers weave the brave and bold.

When the calm begins to grow,
And fierce winds start to slow,
I'll remember every sigh,
Whispers linger, never die.

Symphony of Solitude

In stillness found, a quiet song,
Melodies where I belong.
Notes of silence fill the space,
In solitude, I find my grace.

Each heartbeat marks a gentle theme,
In the hush, I build my dream.
Strings of thought play soft and low,
In the dark, I let them flow.

A tapestry of whispered sighs,
Lifts me up towards the skies.
Within this realm, I feel alive,
In solitude, I truly thrive.

The symphony, a sweet retreat,
In this world, I am complete.
Harmony of heart and mind,
A sacred peace, I always find.

Fragments of Light and Shade

In the twilight, shadows blend,
Lingering light, a gentle friend.
Fragments flicker, dance and play,
In the balance of night and day.

Golden hues on paths of gray,
Whisper secrets that won't stay.
Each moment, a fleeting blend,
In light and shade, we transcend.

Softly weaving through the trees,
Sunlight filters with the breeze.
Every color, every hue,
Captures whispers, old and new.

In the dusk, the world sighs low,
As fragments spark and softly glow.
Finding beauty in the blend,
In light and shade, we make amends.

Illumination through Shadows

In the quiet dark, a flicker exists,
A subtle glow that cannot be missed.
Whispers of light in corners unknown,
Guiding the lost, where seeds have been sown.

Shadows dance as stories unfold,
In the chiaroscuro, truths are retold.
Each beam a promise, each shadow a sigh,
Illumination blooms, as the night draws nigh.

Through veils of doubt, the heart learns to see,
The beauty in chaos, the path that can be.
Fear fades like mist in the morning's embrace,
As light sweeps the darkness, revealing its grace.

With every step taken, hope takes its stand,
In the interplay of night and the hand.
To seek out the light in the thick of despair,
Is to find one's own strength, forever laid bare.

A Spectrum of Tempests

Winds howl fierce with secrets untold,
Colors collide in a storm uncontrolled.
Lightning etches dreams on the canvas of night,
Thunder resounds with a voice full of might.

Rain falls like whispers, soft yet profound,
Dancers of chaos, all swirling around.
Each drop a story, each wave a song,
Together they flourish, uniting the strong.

In the heart of the tempest, courage turns bright,
As rainbows emerge from the rubble of fright.
Nature's own symphony, wild and free,
A spectrum of tempests, in harmony be.

With each passing squall, new colors arise,
In the tapestry woven beneath brooding skies.
Embrace the tumult; let it roar, let it cry,
For within every storm, the soul learns to fly.

Cascade of Conflicting Desires

In the heart's ambivalence, shadows entwine,
Dreams battle realities, from darkness to shine.
Whispers of longing collide in the night,
Each thought a cascade, a flickering light.

Paths intertwine where temptations reside,
Amidst clashing echoes, the heart must decide.
Desires like rivers, both gentle and wild,
Flow through the essence, where fate is beguiled.

Yet still in the currents, the soul seeks its peace,
Amidst clamor and chaos, yearnings increase.
Each drop a reflection of what might be true,
In the midst of the struggle, the self will break through.

With every desire, a lesson unspun,
The dance of conflicting, yet under the sun.
Grow through the tempest, rise high on the crest,
For the heart's deepest wishes lead onward to rest.

Heartbeats in the Maelstrom

In the eye of the storm, where calm meets the chaos,
Heartbeats echo, a rhythm that stays with us.
Riding the waves, each pulse is a guide,
Navigating depths where emotions reside.

The rush of the tempest, both fear and delight,
Weaving together the fabric of night.
In the maelstrom's grasp, let bravery reign,
For through every heartbeat, storm lessons gain.

Roots dig in deeper, both anchored and free,
In the whirlwind's embrace, we learn how to be.
With each crashing heartbeat, a story unfolds,
A testament carved in the courage we hold.

So rise with the tide, let your spirit explore,
Amidst swirling emotions, let your heart roar.
For in this grand dance of life, we find hope,
Heartbeats in the maelstrom help us to cope.

Eye of the Tempest

In the heart where winds collide,
Fear and peace both coincide.
Dark clouds loom, yet light shines near,
In quiet chaos, truth is clear.

Whispers dance upon the breeze,
Nature's symphony with ease.
Time stands still, as spirits soar,
In the eye, we face the roar.

Calm embraces stormy wails,
Hope grows where the tempest hails.
A moment held, then swept away,
In swirling skies, we learn to sway.

Through the turmoil, courage blooms,
In shadows cast by looming glooms.
The tempest's gaze, both fierce and bright,
Guides us home through restless night.

Labyrinth of Turbulence

Winding paths of fear and fate,
Whispers echo, it's not too late.
Twists and turns, a tangled web,
Within each shadow, secrets ebb.

Walls of doubt rise high and tall,
Yet in the dark, we hear the call.
Every corner hides a truth,
Lost in the rush of fleeting youth.

Step by step through stormy night,
Finding solace in the fight.
With every heartbeat, we advance,
In chaos, we learn to dance.

The labyrinth calls, brave hearts respond,
In the maze, we feel so fond.
Through trials faced, we carve a way,
To find the dawn of a new day.

Stormy Serenade

Rainfall whispers muffled songs,
Echoing where each note belongs.
Drums of thunder, a feathery beat,
Nature's rhythm, wild and sweet.

Glimmers flash in the midnight sky,
As lightning dances, spirits fly.
Chaos swells into a tune,
Serenade of the storm at noon.

Melodies born from turbulent skies,
Lift our souls, break all ties.
Harmony found in the squall,
A reminder that we can stand tall.

With every gust, new verses play,
In stormy serenade, we sway.
Lightning hearts and rainswept dreams,
Together we rise with hopeful beams.

Euphoria's Hailstorm

In bursts of joy, the heavens spill,
Hailstones glitter, time stands still.
Each drop a moment, pure delight,
In euphoria's rush, we take flight.

Beneath the storm, we find our ground,
Laughter echoes, a joyful sound.
With every shard that falls around,
Dreams awaken, hope unbound.

Colors clash in a vibrant race,
In fierce delight, we find our place.
The cold embraces, warms the soul,
In the hailstorm, we are whole.

Let the heavens pour their bliss,
In each collision lies a kiss.
Through splendor's veil, we always dare,
In euphoria's storm, love fills the air.